LIVE ON PURPOSE

SAM RICHARDSON JR.

LIVE ON PURPOSE

XULON PRESS

Xulon Press
2301 Lucien Way #415
Maitland, FL 32751
407.339.4217
www.xulonpress.com

© 2019 by Sam Richardson Jr.

All rights reserved solely by the author. The author guarantees all contents are original and do not infringe upon the legal rights of any other person or work. No part of this book may be reproduced in any form without the permission of the author. The views expressed in this book are not necessarily those of the publisher.

All Scripture quotations unless otherwise indicated are taken from the Holy Bible, New International Version, King James Version, or New King James Version as listed on: Biblegateway.com, Bible.org, sermoncentral.org.

Stories and other illustrations were quoted from the following sites: Forbes.com, Charisma.org, Sparkpeople.com, Livingfree.com, ctb.ku.edu, and Everystudent.com.

Printed in the United States of America.

ISBN-13: 978-1-54567-589-2

Contents

Introduction		vii
Chapter One	Why Am I Here?	1
Chapter Two	Purpose Partners	11
Chapter Three	A Twisted Purpose	19
Chapter Four	Fear: The Ultimate Purpose Blocker	29
Chapter Five	Don't Quit	43
Chapter Six	Stay Focused	55
Chapter Seven	Renewing Your Mind	63
Chapter Eight	Living with Expectancy	75

Introduction

One of the age-old questions that silently seep through the tiny, dark crevices of most people's minds is: What is my purpose? Many individuals believe their occupation is synonymous with their purpose—their life's mission. Most are satisfied with this belief until they wake up one day questioning their very existence and find themselves on long rides to nowhere as they try to determine why they were created. You'd be surprised to know how many people wonder why they even entered this world in the first place. Wondering is to put it mildly, but more like obsessing over it. Sometimes it is a dead-end job; no real, meaningful connections or relationships; and no knowledge of purpose that lead folks to believe they have no other reason to be on Earth other than to take up space. They feel that if they disappeared tomorrow, they would easily be replaced by another. It is unfortunate, but, because they have yet to realize just how meaningful their lives are, they are left to sit or stand in awe of someone else's life who appears to have meaning, wield power, and have influence. They trade in the tickets to their own life and would rather relax in the admiration of others' hopes, goals, and dreams.

To the contrary, there are those who feel they are living their purpose simply because their profession has brought them a measurable level of success—those who act as though comfort and luxury are the chief requirements of life. *Luke 12:15b says, "for a man's life consists not in the abundance of the things which he possesses."* Yet, so many individuals falsely appraise their life and their life's value based upon their net worth. The profusion of substance may only survive for a fleeting moment, but a person who knows their purpose understands the brevity of such abundance and will refuse to hinge the summary of their life on the latches thereof. My friends, the truth of the matter is, for us to be truly happy, we must have something to live for. To hope for. To believe in. Show me a man who knows his purpose, and I'll show you a content man.

John W. Gardner, founding chairman of Common Cause, said, "It's a rare and high privilege to help people understand the difference they can make — not only in their own lives, but also in the lives of others, simply by giving of themselves."

Gardner tells of a cheerful old man who asked the same question of just about every new acquaintance he had a conversation with: "What have you done that you believe in and you are proud of?" He never asked conventional questions such as, "What do you do for a living?" It was always, "What have you done that you believe in and are proud of?" It was a disconcerting question for people who had built their self-esteem on their wealth, family name, or their prestigious job title.

Not that the old man was a fierce interrogator, but he was delighted by a woman who answered, "I'm doing a good job raising three children;" by a cabinetmaker who said, "I believe in good workmanship and practice it;" and by a woman who said, "I started a bookstore, and it's the best bookstore for miles around."

"I don't really care how they answer," the old man said. "I just want to put the thought into their minds. They should live their lives in such a way that they can have a good answer. Not a good answer for me, but for themselves. That's what's important."

So, for some what makes life complete is their wealth, but for others it might be a relationship. Without that relationship, there

Introduction

is a void, a vacuum in life. I'm certain you can attest to the emptiness you feel when you have lost someone you loved and held dear to your heart. That sense of loss seems to pervade every part of your life, and no matter what efforts you put into moving forward, the loss holds you hostage in a cell with what can be your worst enemy—your emotions. This sort of imprisonment makes it near to impossible to function in life, let alone your purpose, once again leaving one to question if they have any purpose at all.

H.G. Wells, a famous historian and philosopher, said at age sixty-one: "I have no peace. All life is at the end of the tether." The poet Byron said, "My days are in yellow leaf, the flowers and fruits of life are gone, the worm and the canker, and the grief are mine alone." The literary genius Thoreau said, "Most men live lives of quiet desperation."

Ralph Barton, one of the top cartoonists of the nations, left this note pinned to his pillow before taking his own life: "I have had few difficulties, many friends, great successes; I have gone from wife to wife, from house to house, visited great countries of the world, but I am fed up with inventing devices to fill up twenty-four hours of the day." Oh, my, what an atrocity that is.

Christians without goals are a little like Alice in the fairy tale *Alice in Wonderland*. In a conversation between her and the Cheshire Cat, Alice asked, "Would you tell me please, which way I ought to go from here?"

"That depends a good deal on where you want to get to," said the cat.

"I don't much care where," said Alice.

"Then it doesn't matter which way you go," said the cat.

Wow, can you answer that question? Where do you want to go?

In this book, we are going to cover why you have purpose, where your purpose originated from, who should be involved in your purpose, what your purpose is, and when you should operate in your purpose.

While the conversation of purpose has been had by many, this book will give you a spiritual, practical, and applicable approach to living your life with purpose—on purpose.

Chapter One

Why Am I Here?

In the 1940s, Viktor Frankl was held prisoner in Nazi concentration camps. Imagine this: You, your family, friends, and all your neighbors are all cornered, captured, and transported to mass murdering sites where you're dehumanized and likely extinguished. Frankl lived that reality. He felt the horror of losing everything only to be tortured and terrorized. With all the agony and brutality, what kept Frankl from giving up his relentless fight for his life? It was purpose. He found meaning in his struggle, and that's what gave him the power to push forward through unimaginable pain.

After escaping the concentration camps, Frankl published a book called *Man's Search for Meaning,* which explores his experiences and includes an overview of logotherapy. A quote by Nietzsche nicely sums up his philosophy on how people could survive the camps, without losing the will to live: "He who has a *why* to live for can bear almost any *how.*"

That is the power of purpose. Torture, brutality, unimaginable inhumanity—purpose supersedes it all. Purpose is what gives us the strength to carry on, if not through dire conditions, then through difficult changes, transitions, relationships, and activities.

As Frankl wrote: "In some way, suffering ceases to be suffering at the moment it finds a meaning, such as the meaning of a sacrifice."

Clearly, we live under much different circumstances than Viktor Frankl. Our search for purpose isn't spearheaded by such an extremity. Jacob Sokul suggests when living a *practical* life of purpose, we can see the picture on both a "micro" level and a "macro" level. Your micro level purpose is to *know your values* and, then, *be in integrity with them*. When you know what you stand for and do what you believe in, your confidence and sense of self-worth will be sky-high, regardless of how much the situation sucks. But that's only part of living on purpose. Your macro level purpose is something different. It's the big picture. It's your search for meaning. It's your ultimate goal. It's waking up in the morning knowing you're on the right path, regardless of what other people say.

The notion of one's purpose is inadvertently embedded in us at a very early age. It starts when you are a child. Parents, teachers, and adults in general ask you the nagging question, "So, what do you want to be when you grow up?" If you were the average kid like me, I was grossly confused by the question until I got older. What did they think I wanted to be? The heck if I knew. But that one question had an uncanny way of producing insurmountable pressure as you struggled to come up with something. As with most little boys who grew up during my era, all I was concerned about was acquiring the latest figurine of G.I. Joe or Transformers. I had no clue what I wanted to be, and besides, you could never give them the answer they were looking for anyway. For a question that shouldn't have a right or wrong answer, you would discover that was not the case the moment you said something contrary to what they thought you should say. Most parents wanted you to reply with respectable occupation that would produce an ample salary, and in my case, I think it's safe to say that no parent ever would have applauded a child who said their desire was to be a preacher. I mean, they would probably think it to be cute and would have felt that was a notable profession to enter only if you had a different, "real" job.

That question has resulted in many people today being stuck in positions of employment they despise because they chose it based on the opinions of others. They matriculated in colleges and universities around the world to obtain a career they could hoist their ego on, all while having no interest in it whatsoever. I wonder how many people who are reading this book went to college and didn't decide on a major until your Junior or Senior year, and even then, you selected one because you were forced to. In effort to make Momma proud or Daddy proud, we have people who are financially set on their jobs, but go home at the close of their work day feeling empty, lost, and confused. You will hear them say things like, "There has to be more to life than this." Or, "Am I required to do this for the rest of my life?" Or, "I hate my job. I wish I could do what I really want to do." Perhaps no one has ever told them that, at any moment, they can make a step towards having the life they have only dreamed of.

That intimidating question posed to me as a child is the very reason I encourage parents to nurture their children's gifts and talents. Often, purpose can be embedded within them, and encouraging your child to pursue their passion will prove to be beneficial as they receive their rites of passage into adulthood. Otherwise, those children will grow up to be the adult who questions why they are here.

Let me first say this: if you are breathing, there is a purpose for you here in this world. At any given moment, your last breath can be collected, carried off by the angel of death, and your entire existence will be reduced to a mere memory, and if you found your purpose, your legacy will assume the role of speaking for you since your voice will no longer be heard. Thus, it is vitally important to live on purpose because when this life is over, that's it. There will be no more opportunities to figure it out. There will be no do-overs.

So, let's dive right into your question: Why am I here?

Before I answer that, tell me, why do *you* think you are here? Think about that for a moment. Replay the question in your mind a few times before you arrive at your final answer. Once you have reached your conclusion, I want you to write it down.

Help save the world

Look at your answer. Does your answer include anything you are already doing? Does your answer include you being useful to your family, community, and society at large?

If not, here is a major point I want you to write on a post-it or set as a pop-up reminder on your smart phone:

I'M LIVING WITH THE INTENT TO BE USEFUL.

What if I had never become a preacher? Would I still be operating in my purpose? Absolutely. How so? I am glad you asked. Are you ready for this? Here it is. My purpose is not my profession, but my profession exemplifies and points to what my purpose is. My purpose is to bring insight, inspire, and impact the lives of people. The reason you may be struggling in your profession is because your profession has absolutely nothing to do with your purpose. It is impossible to operate in purpose and remain unsatisfied.

I need you to know and understand this as well. You were not just created to be someone's child, wife, mother, husband, father, sister, or brother. You were not just created to be an employee who works just to pay bills or a CEO who provides jobs to others so they can pay their bills. No. That is a part of your life, and if you are operating in your purpose, it's a very small part of your purpose. I can assure you whatever title you hold, it is not the be-all end-all for your life. There is so much more to you, to life, than that. The problem comes in when you fail to adequately separate who you are from what you do. Until you master this, you will forever be on the treadmill of life—not going anywhere or making any significant progress to reach your desired destination. Here is where I must parenthetically pause to raise the same question as presented in my Introduction:

WHERE ARE YOU GOING?

As a Christian believer, we were created to worship God. The Bible says in Psalm 150:6, "Let everything that has breath praise the Lord. Praise the Lord." Therefore, if you are a breathing, living creature operating in a human body, you have a mandate to give praise to your Creator. If you can find no other viable reason to use your breath, open your mouth, lift your hands, do something that will give praise to God—the giver of life. In my own experience, I have come to realize that during my moments of worship, I'm reminded of why God created me. There is nothing like being in the presence of God, the one who created you, and allowing Him to breathe afresh on you so that the purpose in which you were created can be stirred up, renewed, and refreshed. I would submit to you that when you are in doubt—worship. When you have questions—worship. When your purpose doesn't make sense, and it doesn't align with where you are in life—worship. I can even validate this for you in scripture. Psalm 16:11 declares, "You will make known to me the path of life; in your presence is the fullness of joy; in your right hand, there are pleasures forever."

So, let's look at this verse.

It begins with the writer affirming the point I just made. In His presence, you get a three-for-one special. One, you get clarity on your purpose; two, you get the fullness of joy; and, three, you get pleasures. I know it has become cliché to say, but, what a mighty God we serve. Where else can you go, or who can you run to, that will give you everything you need and a lot of what you want? Beloved, before you spend another day vacillating with yourself about what you should be doing, and how you should be doing it, find some time to worship. Before you cry another tear or spend priceless moments being depressed, find some time to barge into God's presence.

I read an interesting analogy on the hammer and the nail. Consider a hammer. It's designed to hit nails. That's what it was created to do. Now imagine that the hammer never gets used. It just sits in the toolbox. The hammer doesn't care. But, imagine that same hammer with a soul, a self-consciousness. Days and days go by with him remaining in the toolbox. He feels funny inside, but he's not sure exactly why. Something is missing, but he doesn't know what it is. Then, one day, someone pulls him out of the toolbox and uses him to break some branches for the fireplace. The hammer is exhilarated. Being held, being wielded, hitting the branches—the hammer loves it. At the end of the day, though, he is still unfulfilled. Hitting the branches was fun, but it wasn't enough. Something is still missing.

In the days that follow, he's used often. He reshapes a hubcap, blasts through some sheet rock, knocks a table leg back into place. Still, he's left unfulfilled. So, he longs for more action. He wants to be used as much as possible to knock things around, to break things, to blast things, to dent things. He figures that he just hasn't had enough of these events to satisfy him. More of the same, he believes, is the solution to his lack of fulfillment.

One day, someone uses him on a nail. Suddenly, the lights come on in his hammer soul. He now understands what he was truly designed for. He was meant to hit nails. All the other things he hit pale in comparison. Now he knows what his hammer soul was searching for all along.

We are created in God's image for relationship with Him. Being in that relationship is the only thing that will ultimately satisfy our souls. Until we come to know God, we may have had many wonderful experiences, but we haven't hit a nail. We've been used for some noble purposes, but not the one we were ultimately designed for, not the one through which we will find the most fulfillment. Augustine summarized it this way: "You [God] have made us for yourself and our hearts are restless until they find their rest in Thee."

A relationship with God is the only thing that will quench our soul's longing. Jesus Christ said, "I am the bread of life. He who comes to me will never go hungry, and he who believes in me will never be thirsty." Until we come to know God, we are hungry and thirsty in life. We try to "eat" and "drink" all kinds of things to satisfy our hunger and thirst, yet they remain.

We are like the hammer. We don't realize what will end the emptiness, the lack of fulfillment, in our lives. Even during a Nazi prison camp, Corri Ten Boom found God to be wholly satisfying: "The foundation of our happiness was that we knew ourselves hidden with Christ in God. We could have faith in God's love... our Rock who is stronger than the deepest darkness."

Usually when we keep God out, we try to find fulfillment in something other than God, but we can never get enough of that thing. We keep "eating" or "drinking" more and more, erroneously thinking that 'more' is the answer to the problem, yet we are never ultimately satisfied. Our greatest desire is to know God, to have a relationship with God. Why? Because that's how we've been designed. Have you hit a nail yet?

I promised you this book would be filled with applicable tips for you to lead a more purpose-filled life. So, here is a practical tip worth notating*:* ***Let go of thinking there is only one purpose for you and embrace the idea that our purpose in life is to love life fully by placing ourselves into our life.*** This means we jump in and try new things; we stop resisting the unknown, and we fully engage in what is happening right here, where we are. I mentioned this before, but it's worth another mention; lead a purposeful life, follow your passions. When we live a passion-filled life, we are living on purpose, and that is the purpose of life. That feeling that something is missing goes away when you lead a passion-filled life. The need to seek our purpose comes from a lack of passion. When you don't feel connected to your life, you lack purpose and passion. To help cure this emptiness, simply add more passion.

Your heart is typically the best means to access your true purpose and passion. Ask yourself what you love. Start taking steps to do what you love. When you are inspired and connected to your content self, inspiration deluges your heart and soul. When you lead from your heart, you are naturally more ecstatic and inspired to explore. By doing what you love, you will be moved and gain insight into what brings you the most joy.

So, here is a quick recap of the top three points of this chapter:

1) Gifts and talents produce passion.
2) When passion matures, it produces purpose.
3) Without a relationship with God, one's purpose will never be known.

Now, taking into consideration what we've gone over in this chapter, let me rephrase the childhood question and ask, "What are your passions? How are you using them to help you live your purpose?" Write your answers below.

Why Am I Here?

Exercise, health, self awareness, meditation, exploring one self in a healthy way. Helping others purely, being able to keep my ears plugged but know I am help & goal for this Earth as are others. Exploring trust, talking, more listening, peace, questions, fasting, prayer, forgiveness, focus, drive, breathing, risk.

Chapter Two

Purpose Partners

You will not be able to live on purpose and in your purpose, if you have the wrong people around you.

Sometimes the wrong person isn't the one you are romantically linked to. Sometimes the wrong person can be an immediate family member. Whatever the case, you cannot afford to be attached to people who pose an imminent threat to you living the life God purposed for you to live. You must arrive at a place within yourself where you have no qualms saying farewell to those who are no longer going in the same direction as you. The reality is, toxic and unhealthy relationships and the drama they bring, cause more damage than anything else. These types of relationships are like a cancer that infuses its way into your destiny and slowly begins to chip away at it. You may not notice a difference instantly, and you may even brush it off, opting to deal with it later; but before long, you will find yourself wondering what happened to your drive, your motivation, your faith, and your belief that you are were born and created for something magnificent. You will know you are in good company if the company you keep is constantly pushing you to greatness and challenging you to be better even if you think you have already made it. The wrong company will do the exact opposite and cause you to question the things you know God has said about you.

Here is the first takeaway point of this chapter:

> **EVERYBODY IS NOT GOING TO LIKE YOU.**

You got that? I need that to settle into the fissures of your spirit. No matter how fascinating you may believe you are, some people just won't find you enthralling. Some people are going to find fault in everything you do. For some people, you will never be enough, and nothing you do will be good enough. There will be people who will love being around you if you are not a threat to their little kingdom. They will like you if they feel better and bigger than you. But, once God begins to bless you with something they wish they had, then the problems ensue. And, that is okay. That's not your problem to be concerned with. If you want everybody to like you, then you are pretty going to have to resolve to not going anywhere and not having anything. More people are not living their life of purpose because they are more concerned with what others are thinking about them or not thinking about them. You will never get anywhere in life if you are waiting for everyone to join hands with you and help you get where you are trying to go. There must be a built-in determination that drives you even if you must go alone.

Despite the naysayers, you must keep going towards the goal line. And, you know what, as I kept going, God sent people who every now and then jumped on the field to offer a towel, a word of encouragement, and even a push when I felt like giving up. When you are living on purpose, those are the type of people it is imperative you be surrounded by.

The definition of the word friend varies from person to person, and depending on that person, it's possible for them to have a distorted view as to what it means to be a friend. There was a time when being referred to as someone's friend meant something.

Nowadays, you should be extremely mindful of who you consider a friend. In our society, your "friend" may be friends with your enemy. Loyalty is scarce among friendships today, thus you should be more concerned with finding individuals who are associated with your purpose. Those who are connected to your purpose don't take the connection lightly, and they don't take you for granted.

"Purpose Partners" are those who are divinely sent by God to help you live in your purpose. They are those who are not intimidated by the visions God gives you and aren't behind the scenes secretly wishing for your downfall. They aren't the ones who are vying for a position in your life; they are there to help you carry out an assignment. Purpose Partners may not hang out with you on the weekends. They may not come over for holiday dinners. They may not sit in the box with you at sporting events, but they are there when it's time to do something in conjunction with your purpose. These are the people who are willing to jump in where needed, and, even if they don't get public recognition for the work they do, they remain faithful to their purpose which is to serve your purpose. And in today's times, that is huge because there are people who live to see how many likes they can get on Facebook, double-taps they can get on Instagram, and retweets on Twitter.

Second takeaway point:

> **FIND YOUR PURPOSE PARTNERS.**

One of my favorite biblical examples of Purpose Partners is that of David and Jonathan. The Bible reads in I Samuel 18:1-4, *"After David had finished talking with Saul, Jonathan became one in spirit with David, and he loved him as himself. From that day Saul kept David with him and did not let him return home to his family. And Jonathan made a covenant with David because he loved him as himself. Jonathan took off the robe he was wearing and gave it to David, along with his tunic, and even his sword, his bow and his belt."*

Identifying Purpose Partners

➢ **Purpose Partners are linked to your spirit.** The scripture says Jonathan became one in spirit with David. It's great to have friends, but friends may not necessarily be linked to your spirit. Don't believe me? Do something that a friend isn't fond of and see if that thing will withstand the test of the friendship. You can be friends with someone today—hanging out at the mall, shopping, dining—and fall out of that same friendship by nightfall. Friends will walk away. Friends may decide they don't need you anymore, but Purpose Partners are joined to your spirit with spiritual ties that are stronger than fleshly ties and aren't easily broken. It is tremendously easier to remove someone from your life than it is removing them from your spirit. Thereby, if a Purpose Partner is linked to your spirit, whatever is conceived in your spirit (purpose related), they are immediately attached to it and will ensure that you give birth to it. Their only question is, "How can I help?"

➢ **Purpose Partners will take risks with you even if it puts them at risk.** David and Jonathan were what we would consider today best friends. Jonathan was so knitted to David's purpose that he was willing to risk his own life if necessary. Jonathan went against his own father, King Saul, and told David, whatever he needed him to do, he would do it. *(Read I Samuel 20:1-42.)* Don't miss the dynamics of this. Saul, who was initially fond of David, eventually loathed David, and his own son, Jonathan, was willing to lose his life so that David's life could be spared. Do you have any people in your life who are willing to delay, let alone give up, their own dreams, goals, and desires to make sure your purpose is fulfilled? Not only was Jonathan willing to risk his life, but he also came up with a plan to save his life. Let that marinate. A Purpose Partner will help you strategize, so you can identify the many options that are available for you to be successful. Imagine if a football team only had one coach and that coach was responsible for designing plays, calling plays, and watching the field to make sure the plays were executed. There would be a lot fewer people gunning to be coaches if that much pressure was on their shoulders. Such as the same for a person with purpose. A lot less people would be willing to live in their purpose, no matter how much they may want to, if they had to do everything alone. Third takeaway point: **YOU CAN'T DO IT BY YOURSELF.** A Purpose Partner gets in the huddle with you and helps you strategize for the win even if they don't get the praise for it. What is a coach without a defensive or offensive coordinator? What is a purpose without Purpose Partners?

> **Purpose Partners are givers.** When Jonathan made the decision to be in covenant with David, the Scripture says he took off his robe, his tunic, his sword, bow, belt. Wow, what a gesture to make. Most of us have trouble getting people to spend a dollar with our new business, let alone make a sacrifice to give us what we need even if they themselves need it. It is for certain Jonathan could have replaced those garments and weapons, but the notable thing here is that he took it off immediately upon seeing the need, and gave it away. Purpose Partners don't wait to think about *if* they are going to give, they give to the cause right away void of hesitation. I believe it is safe to assume Jonathan's robe

and tunic were crafted and stitched with the most expensive fabrics and threads. He was the son of the king. This would be equivalent to a woman giving away her brand-new Louis Vuitton bag or a man giving away his brand-new pair of Jordans. Not too likely to happen. However, there was no reluctance in him taking it off and handing it over. He did it with joy and gladness. Why? Because he was in covenant—because he was linked to David's purpose. Purpose Partners have an innate desire to see you have all you need to be effective in your purpose. Even if it delays their gratification.

My friends, you cannot fulfill purpose without Purpose Partners. It is time for you to do an evaluation of the people in your circle. It is time to say goodbye to anyone who isn't contributing positively to your life. No book, pastor, preacher, teacher, or life coach can convince you to do this until you get to a point where the relationship is no longer worth it if it means sacrificing another moment of your destiny. When God is going to do something new in your life, whether it be going to the next level of your destiny, bring Purpose Partners on board, or taking you into a season of prosperity; God will often lead you to a place where cuts must take place. The same way everybody cannot make the basketball team, everyone can't go with you all the way.

That is my final takeaway point of this chapter:

- **EVERYBODY CAN'T GO.**

When God was going to do something in Moses's life, He called him to the back side of the desert. When Jacob was at the point of change in his life, he found himself alone wrestling with God. Everybody will not be able to go where God is going to take you. Everybody will not be able to hear what

God is about to speak to you. Everybody will not be able to see what God is about to show you. Some people will not be able to handle the blessings and prosperity God is about to give you. Therefore, God is taking you to a place where the crowd cannot follow. Where the doubters will have no room. Where the haters are irrelevant. The cuts are necessary because He is positioning you for greater, and if you are not careful, people will mess you up. You can't blame the devil for what you can handle yourself. It's time to rid yourself of the people who subtract but don't add. Those who divide but do not multiply. Such folks will slow your progress and hinder you from getting where you need to be, when you need to be there. If they can't handle what God is doing, they are not your Purpose Partners, and they need to go. Now. Keep in mind that the closer Jesus got to the cross, more and more people began to lie on Him, persecute Him, and forsake Him. Even some of His disciples.

When Joseph was born, his brothers had no problem with him. It wasn't until they realized he was their father's favorite when their father gave Joseph the coat of many colors, did they become full of jealousy and envy. Matters grew worse when Joseph began to share his dreams with them. They couldn't handle it and perhaps one of the reasons was because they themselves didn't have a vision or a dream. Some people have no issues with you until you decide that being average no longer suits you and your desire is to be great. Purpose Partners will be elated by that declaration. They are eager to celebrate and rejoice with you. They are fulfilled when they are invited to the victory celebration. They are elated when the promotion comes. Why? Because a win for you is a win for the entire time team.

Beloved, you must resolve that your purpose is not attached to anyone who is willing to walk away from you. If they walk away, I would admonish you to host a going away party. You don't need anyone in your life who can easily walk away. Do not beg people to stay in your life. Do not beg people to be your friend or care about you. Stop trying to force people to share your dreams and visions. No matter their relation to you, what your history with them might be, or what they have done for you in the past; if they need to go, then in as many languages as you know, you need to wish them goodbye. The Bible says in, I John 2:19, *"They went out from us, but they were not of us; for if they had been of us, they would no doubt have continued with us: but they went out, that they might be made manifest that they were not all of us."* Purpose partners walk on the same level with you. They have the same spirit as you. They *do not* walk away. I love how Bishop T. D. Jakes says, "The gift of goodbye is the 10th spiritual gift."

    To receive all God has for you, to live on purpose, you need to be in the proper position and surrounded by the right people. People who may have started with you but are no longer with you may not necessarily be bad people. It just signifies their part of your story has concluded, which means you need to stop trying to extend their presence. Ever been watching a movie and a scene goes on and on and on? Isn't it irritating that you are forced to wait for the scene to end before a new scene can be introduced? Nothing will thrust me into an abyss of boredom faster than watching a movie that is slow to build or change scenes. So, the same way you wouldn't want to watching a boring movie, why would you continue trying to hold on to the person who clearly wants, and needs, to go?

    Always remember that the enemy's most successful entry point into the life of a believer is through another person. So, guard your world. Guard your purpose. While Jesus preached to the multitudes, He had seventy disciples, twelve of the seventy were considered His chosen, and only three were truly a part of His inner circle. Purpose Partners don't always consist of many people, but they are always the chosen people.

Chapter Three

A Twisted Purpose

What do you do when your purpose doesn't seem to make sense? When it's not popular? When it doesn't appear acceptable to the masses? Can you push beyond the expectations of people and adapt your purpose to invoke change in people who are not like you or who don't look like you?

This world we live in is filled with diverse individuals. No two people are alike and, if you are going to operate and live in your purpose, you must understand, and accept, there will be people who were not raised like you. There will be people who do not believe what you believe. There will be people who won't think like you. And the worst thing you can do is limit the vision for your purpose based on it reaching only the demographics that are comfortable for you. I'm sure you've heard it said that only those who live outside of the box go on to do extraordinary things. Very few can be great by continually sitting in the seat of average. Greatness takes place on the wings of risk.

I once preached a sermon titled, "A Twisted Purpose." It was taken from the story of the Canaanite woman who cried out to Jesus to help her daughter. Let's look at that text found in Matthew 15:21-28 (NIV):

Leaving that place, Jesus withdrew to the region of Tyre and Sidon. A Canaanite woman from that vicinity came to him, crying out, "Lord, Son of David, have mercy on me! My daughter is demon-possessed and suffering terribly." Jesus did not answer a word. So his disciples came to him and urged him, "Send her away, for she keeps crying out after us." He answered, "I was sent only to the lost sheep of Israel." The woman came and knelt before him. "Lord, help me!" she said. He replied, "It is not right to take the children's bread and toss it to the dogs." "Yes it is, Lord," she said. "Even the dogs eat the crumbs that fall from their master's table." Then Jesus said to her, "Woman, you have great faith! Your request is granted." And her daughter was healed at that moment.

Before we discuss the great faith of this woman, let's look at the problem with this text.

This woman's daughter was demon-possessed, and those demons were tormenting her. Somewhere, somebody told her Jesus could fix whatever problem she had. So, she did what any terrified mother would do in her situation—she sought help. No one can even blame her for doing this. When a mom is on a mission for the sake of her child, there is not much that will stop her. Moms find the courage to do things they would not normally do to get help for a sick child. So, the Syrophoenician woman sees Jesus, and she does the only thing she can do—she speaks her truth. But, Jesus, does something very strange. He ignores her.

Yes, this is the same compassionate Jesus who had been healing the sick and performing miracles. This is the same Jesus who had been preaching to the multitudes, but because she was from the "other side of the tracks" if you will, He ignored her. So, to put it simply, Jesus didn't want to help her because of where she was from. Bible scholars have tried to present commentary to soften up this text, because it is difficult to digest that Jesus would be so harsh; but the directness of the text is plain for all to see. Jesus calls the woman in the scripture, the "Canaanite woman." The Promised Land that Moses led the Israelites to was Canaan, so the Jews and the Canaanites were historically enemies. But the name Canaan was no longer on the map – Sidon and Tyre were now in the region known as Phoenicia. Some have argued that in this moment Jesus was exemplifying racist behavior. I don't know that I would go as far as to say that, but what is for certain is that He boxed Himself in, believing His purpose was only for a certain group of people. I wonder how many folks reading this book are looking at their purpose through those same lenses? Is your purpose prejudice to only people who come from the same stock as you? The truth of the matter is that everybody has a story. Some were born here. Others were not. Some are old. Others are young. Some are healthy, some are sick. Some are struggling to make ends meet. Some live in abundance. Some were raised in the church. Others are newfound converts. Some are Democrats. Others are Republicans. Transformation happens when we listen to someone else's story that doesn't fit with our narrative or understanding and are challenged as to what we believe, and how we should respond.

If you know anything about a woman, nothing frustrates her more than being ignored. Yet, the mother kept crying out to Jesus. To her dismay, He continued to be silent. What do you do when you are trying to do what you are supposed to be doing yet heaven is quiet? Who do you turn to when Jesus Himself turns a deaf ear? I'll tell you what you do. You allow your purpose to push you to keep fighting until you get what you need. Her need kept her crying. Her daughter's well being kept her nagging. Her desires kept her irritating the Master until He had a change of her heart. The disciples, who grew frustrated with hearing the woman's nagging plea, went to Jesus and said, "Hey, do something to get this woman to shut up." She was getting on their nerves, and she wasn't even talking to them. My friends, that is the same tenacity you will need to live on purpose. When you are trying to live on purpose, you've got to develop a by-any-means-necessary attitude. You've got to do what you must do no matter who likes it or whose nerves you get on, because absolutely nothing comes to the person who gives up. In this case, not even the disciples could get her to shut up. She didn't care that His boys were looking at her strange and giving her the side eye. She maintained her persistence.

Finally, Jesus answered. But it's not just any answer. He replied with a derogatory statement comparing her to a dog. In that day, dogs were wild animals, and it was an insult to refer to any person as a dog, let alone a woman. Nonetheless, he made the statement, saying, "It is not good to take the children's bread and toss it to dogs." Wow! This is Jesus we are talking about. Jesus, who came into the world to call to repentance and save sinners, to present Himself as a ransom for every person no matter who you are, to be a light, to proclaim and preach the good news, to serve as a demonstration of God's love, and to be the Savior of the world. This is that same Jesus. That was His purpose, yet, here He was stuck between the walls of tradition and hypocrisy.

But instead of this woman getting emotional and turning away at His statement, she claims her dignity and courageously gives her view on His actions. She could have easily gone back home to her troubled child and prayed for the best. She could have made an irrational decision like many tend to do when they are driven by their emotions. She could have gotten irate with Jesus and called to question His power. But, she kept her cool, and quietly replied, "Yes, but even the dogs get the crumbs." She essentially said, "I admit that I am no more than a dog, Jesus. But even little dogs are granted mercy from their masters' table. Even they are permitted to eat the scraps that fall from their children's plates. So, I don't believe you will do nothing more for me, Jesus, because I know you are merciful. I've heard how you've helped other Gentiles. I've heard about the mercy you've shown for your people. I believe in your Gospel, and so I refuse to believe that you will not help me in my distress just as your Father helped the Syrian widow and her son (1 Kings 17:67-24) and helped Naaman the leper (2 Kings 5:1-19) through the prophet Elisha."

She, with one statement, asks Him to see things from her perspective. She asks to be treated at least as well as the dogs. And here, the stage is set for an astounding reversal. Surely here we meet the climactic focus of this story, that wondrously-strange and persistent faith that stands its ground against all opposition. This woman is not to be put off, and against all the signs of apparent hopelessness, doggedly stands her ground, persistently seeking the Lord's help, even if it is only to be in those meager crumbs that might fall from the "master's" table. And in the wonderful surprise that is the miracle of faith, she meets the gracious healing power of God's Messiah.

I think that there is something of her in all of us. There are times in our lives when we feel excluded and on the outside, times when we are desperate and fighting for hope, times when we recognize our powerlessness. Times when we are sick or worried about war, world hunger, poverty; when we have feelings of being lost, sad, angry, or fearful and a sense of helplessness in a country that is clearly divided. But, those who are living on purpose will not see these concerns as an opportunity to isolate but will find an opportunity to become adaptable to serve anyone who encounters their purpose-driven life.

Those crumbs from the table are for somebody, and they are not insignificant. God doesn't leave anyone out no matter who they are. Even if that someone is outside of His will, they are not outside the circle of God's love and care. Like this story of the woman who, as an outsider experiences God's mercy and so challenges a too-narrow tradition that would want to restrict God's mercies to a chosen few, these sayings invite a reexamination of our hearts and call us to a new appraisal of our own purpose.

Here is how we relate and implement the above story into our modern-day context.

Relationships are powerful. Our one-to-one connections with each other are the foundation for change. And building relationships with people from different cultures, *often many different cultures*, is key in building diverse communities that are powerful enough to achieve significant goals. Whether you want to make sure your children get a good education, bring quality health care into your communities, or promote economic development, there is a good chance you will need to work with people from several different racial, language, ethnic, or economic groups. And to work with people from different cultural groups effectively, you will need to build sturdy and caring relationships based on trust, understanding, and shared goals.

Why? Because trusting relationships are the glue that hold people together as they work on a common problem. As people work on challenges, they must hang in there together when things get hard. They must support each other to stay with an effort, even when it feels discouraging. People must resist the efforts of those who use divide-and-conquer techniques—pitting one cultural group against another.

Whether you are African American, Caucasian, Asian, Hispanic, Catholic, Jewish, or from any other racial, ethnic, religious, or socioeconomic group, you will probably need to establish relationships with people whose group you may know very little about. Each one of us is like a hub of a wheel. Each one of us can build relationships and friendships around ourselves that provide us with the necessary strength to achieve goals. If each person builds a network of diverse and strong relationships, we can come together and solve complications that we have in common.

It appeared that Jesus's purpose in the story was twisted because He had not considered crossing certain boundaries in His ministry, but by doing so, the Apostle Paul later writes in Romans 10:12 (NIV), *"For there is no difference between Jew and Gentile—the same Lord is Lord of all and richly blesses all who call on Him."* What if Jesus had not first set the example?

That said, here are some ways you can get out of the box and embrace people who are not like you so you can maximize your purpose.

- **Make a conscious decision to establish friendships with people from other cultures.**

Deciding is the first step. To build relationships with people different from yourself, you have to make a concerted effort to do so. There are societal forces that serve to separate us from each other. People from different economic groups, religions, ethnic groups, and races are often isolated from each other in schools, jobs, and neighborhoods. So, if we want things to be different, we need to take active steps to make them different. Once you have made the decision to make friends with people different from yourself, you can go ahead and make friends with them in much the same way as with anyone else. You may need to take more time, and you may need to be more persistent. You may need to reach out and take the initiative more than you are used to. People who have been mistreated by society may take more time to trust you than people who haven't. Don't let people discourage you. There are good reasons why people have built up defenses, but it is not impossible to overcome them and make a connection. The effort is worth it.

- **Examine your biases about people from different cultures.**

We all carry misinformation and stereotypes about people in different cultures. Especially, when we are young, we acquire this information in bits and pieces from TV, from listening to people talk, and from the culture at large. We are not bad people because we acquired this; no one requested to be misinformed. But to build relationships with people of different cultures, we must become aware of the misinformation we acquired. People, for the most part, want to be asked questions about their lives and their cultures. Many of us were told that asking questions was nosy; but if we are thoughtful, asking questions can help you learn about people of different cultures and help build relationships. People are usually pleasantly surprised when others show interest in *their* cultures. If you are sincere and willing to listen, people will tell you a lot. For example, you might ask a person of African heritage if they want to be called black or African-American. Or you can ask a Jewish person what it is like for them at Christmas time when practically every store, TV commercial, and radio station focuses almost entirely on Christmas.

- **Don't forget to care.**

It is easy to forget that the basis of any relationship is caring. Everyone wants to care and be cared about. Caring about people is what makes a relationship real. Don't let your awkwardness around cultural differences get in the way of caring about people.

- **Listen to people tell their stories.**

If you get an opportunity to hear someone tell you her life story first hand, you can learn a lot—and build a strong relationship at the same time. *Every* person has an important story to tell. Each person's story tells something about their culture. Listening to people's stories, we can get a fuller picture of what people's lives are like—their feelings, their nuances, and the richness of their lives. Listening to people also helps us get through our numbness; there is a real person before us, not someone who is reduced to stereotypes in the media. Additionally, listening to members of groups that have been discriminated against can give you a better understanding of what that experience is like. Listening gives us a picture of discrimination that is more real than what we can get from reading or by listening to a third party's account.

In conclusion, our job is not to criticize, reject, or judge. Our purpose is to offer a helping hand, compassion, and mercy. As we have all been taught, the Golden Rule is for us to do unto others as we want things done unto us. My brothers and sisters of all nationalities, let us learn to work together for the common cause of fulfilling our purpose in the Earth.

Chapter Four

Fear: The Ultimate Purpose Blocker

Once you discover what your purpose is, the next thing you must do is start living it.

I know you're thinking that is easier said than done, but if you don't decide to do it, you will eventually fall into a doubt trap that will entangle you in procrastination. Before long, months will have passed, and the next thing you know, it will be years later, and you will still be talking about what you are going to do versus doing it.

What if the time isn't right? What if living on purpose requires you to abandon your current way of thinking, your current way of living, or your current way of surviving? Those are all questions commonly asked by individuals who are vacillating with the idea of making a move towards living on purpose. Let me ask you this: What do you have to lose? If you are not living on purpose, chances are you are unhappy anyway, and what is your happiness worth to you?

You may have noticed that as you get older, time seems to move faster. Summers are shorter you often run behind and spend more time than ever before catching up. No matter how we perceive the passing of time, the fact is, that the clock is ticking. Every moment that you don't get started, is a moment that passes you by. This is not to say you should always be busy, but isn't it time to stop waiting for the perfect time?

If you aren't ready to get started, figure out what is holding you back from taking the first step. Fear of failure? Fear of looking silly? Laziness? Depression? What could be scarier than living a life that passed you by? What could be worse than going day to day feeling uninspired, unmotivated, and stuck. Feeling silly, facing fear, and being a little crazy will help you choose to change. Admit it, embrace it, fix it, and move forward. This is the right time, your perfect moment to start living *life on purpose*.

So, let's talk about fear—the ultimate purpose blocker.

Fear is the most powerful single factor that deprives you of being able to achieve your full potential. You experience it most often because of your own thoughts and emotional visions, rather than actual real-world causes. In other words, you become fearful of a fantasy – something that doesn't exist.

Fear is a cloaked enemy that whispers negative thoughts into your mind, body, and soul. It tries to convince you that you will not succeed and that you cannot achieve your full potential. These thoughts are lies.

The road you are traveling may be a bit scary at times, but don't lose faith. Don't listen to your fears and the fears of those around you. Don't let old setbacks work their way into your present thinking. And most of all, don't give up on what's important to you.

It's fine to feel a bit uncomfortable. It's okay if you don't know exactly what's going to happen next or how much you can handle. If you gradually step forward, you will learn what you need to know. You will let go of the scary things that 'might happen' and start to see all the great realities unfolding around you.

This is your life and it's an open road. Grab the wheel with both hands and keep steering yourself around all the unnecessary fears and uncertainties as they arise. Here's how:

1. Envision and declare what you want.

Regardless of fear or actual real-world barriers, whenever you want to achieve something, you must envision it and declare it. You must keep your eyes open and focused specifically on what you want. It's simply impossible to hit a target you haven't declared, or get anywhere worthwhile with your eyes closed or your vision blurred.

The first step is realizing that what you want to achieve is already a big part of who you are. You may be a novice just beginning a great journey, or you may be a veteran who hasn't yet realized her dream. Either way, the fact that you haven't attained your desired result yet doesn't make you any less of a force to be reckoned with.

In other words, if you want to run a marathon, you are a marathon runner. You just need to run. If you want to be a writer, you are a writer. You just need to write. It's only ever a matter of training, studying, and practicing.

Whatever it is you want to do, envision it and declare it out loud: "I am going to _____."

2. Know the consequence of staying where you are.

What would life be if we had no courage to attempt anything? It wouldn't be. Life is movement. Inaction based on fear not only stops you from achieving, it stops you from living.

Your future depends on what you do today. The fear of failure, or whatever, can be daunting, but it's nowhere near as bad as the realization of looking back on great opportunities you never took. Don't be satisfied with telling stories others have lived. Write your own story, your way.

3. Believe.

What you believe either weakens you or makes you stronger. If you want to give yourself the best gift you could ever receive, believe in yourself.

The foundation of the success you desire is not based on being in a certain place, at a certain level of achievement, or a combination of external factors; it is simply a mindset. Success is an attitude that comes from powerful beliefs and empowering thoughts. What you think and believe about your life directly determines how you feel, what actions you take, and what you ultimately achieve.

Believing takes practice, but it also makes the impossible possible. Is it worth the effort? Absolutely!

4. Take it slow, but GO!

Yes, take a step, and another. Keep going! Achievement involves lots of doing. What you achieve is based on what you believe *and* what you act upon, not just what you believe. You've got to take your beliefs and put persistent effort into them.

There is no progress without action. What is not started today is never finished by tomorrow. Some of the greatest ideas and dreams die young. Why? Because the genius behind the idea or dream fails to *go* forward with it – they think about it, but never *do* anything about it.

Just remember, no action always results in a 100 percent failure rate. So, get into action now and begin moving in the right direction. After you get started every step thereafter gets easier and easier, until what once had seemed light years away is suddenly standing right in front of you.

5. Accept that failure is possible and necessary.

As Winston Churchill once said, "Success is stumbling from failure to failure with no loss of enthusiasm."

Failure is necessary. On the path toward success, you may encounter many failures, but *you* are not a failure. Failures are simply stepping stones that slowly uncover the correct path forward, one slippery step at a time. You can't get anywhere without these steps.

So, don't wake up at eighty years of age, sighing over what you should have tried but didn't because you were scared to fail. Just do it and be willing to fail and learn along the way. Very few people get it right on the first shot. In fact, most people fail to get it right on the first twenty shots. If what you did today didn't turn out as you had hoped, tomorrow is a new opportunity to try again and build upon what you've learned.

And remember, in the end, the greatest thing about your journey is not so much where you stand at any given time, as it is about what direction you're moving. Your fears are not as scary as you think, and they're not here to stop you. They're here to let you know that what you want is worth fighting for.

One of the most majestic of all creatures is the tiger. For many years, these big, beautiful creatures have puzzled researchers. It seems that when tigers hunt, they have a remarkable capacity for causing their prey to paralyze with fear, a capacity greater than any of the other big cats. As the tiger charges toward its ill-fated prey it lets out a spine-chilling roar. You'd think this would be enough to cause the prey to turn and run for its life, but instead, it often freezes and soon becomes the tiger's food.

At the turn of this century, scientists at the Fauna Communication Research Institute in North Carolina discovered why you're likely to freeze rather than run when a tiger charges. When the tiger roars, it lets out sound waves that are audible – the ones that sound terrifying – and it also lets out sound at a frequency so low you can't hear it, but you can feel it. And so, as the tiger emerges from the undergrowth, the flashing of its colors; the sound of its roar; and the impact of the unheard, but felt, sound waves combine to provide an all-out assault on your senses. The effect is that you are momentarily paralyzed, so even though there may be time to avoid the tiger, you are tricked into standing still long enough for the tiger to leap on you.

Our fears often operate in the same way. They paralyze us into inactivity, even when the real threat is not immediately upon us. Part of overcoming the challenges before us is to recognize the ability for our fear of what might happen to stop us from dealing with the challenge.

So, how do we deal with fear when you are trying to live on purpose? Let's look at a couple of ways.

➢ **Feel**

> Our first point of recognizing emotion is seeing where the physiological changes occur within our body. Note where in the body you are feeling a reaction, "I'm feeling tightness in my chest." From there. observe what the chatter is in your head, what are you thinking? From there, label what emotion you are feeling, "I am feeling tightness in my chest. I had the thought that I can't do this." Then breathe. Take a few deep breaths, leaning into the fear. Soothing your soul. Calming your mind. Breathe into the fear.

➢ **Elevate**

> Get bigger than your fear! When we are in the midst of having an emotion, our body language changes. We feel fear, and then we turn inward, hunching over, crossing legs,

protecting ourselves from the perceived threat. Therefore, you must do whatever needs to be done to counteract that feeling. Clap your hands. Stomp your feet. Be bigger than the fearful voice inside.

➢ Action

As Nike would say, "Just do it!" Move forward in life, push through the resistance, and do the task you fear the most. Create new evidence that you can do things that are a success. Note all the good things in your life, all your achievements, and all the positive things you have already created. Take note of the fear and push through. Do what you fear the most. Only then can you grow and learn as a human being. Only then can you step into your light and own your power.

➢ Respond

Be kind to yourself. Speak with loving words. Understand where your fear is coming from and what you are believing about yourself to be the truth. Loving yourself heals. Compassion changes both yourself and those around you.

It can be a scary thing, chasing your dreams. The fear of leaving behind what you have always known to embrace the unknown. When we push through fear, we shred old beliefs, destroy past patterns, and change limiting thoughts. Feel the fear and move forward anyway. Acknowledge it, lean into the physiological responses, breathe deeply, and go for it. At the end of the day, see yourself as a scared little child seeking reassurance and comfort. Provide yourself with loving compassion and firmly say, "We are going to do this."

Faith, as you may know, is the antidote to fear. Sometimes the only way to discover God's will is to practice stepping out and finding out. If I have prayed about a situation and don't seem to know what I should do, I take a step of faith. I know that trusting God is like standing before the automatic door at the grocery store. You can stand and look at the door all day long, but it will remain closed until you take a step forward and trigger the mechanism that opens the door. Don't spend your life in so much fear of making a mistake that you never do anything. Scripture says, "For God has not given us a spirit of fear, but of power and of love and of a sound mind" (2 Tim. 1:7, NKJV). You cannot drive a parked car. You need to be moving if you want God to show you which way to go. He leads one step at a time. If you take one step forward in the wrong direction, He will let you know before you go too far.

I often think of Joshua, a man who was given a huge task by God – one I'm sure he didn't feel ready for. Can you imagine how he felt when Moses died and God told him that *he* was going to take over and lead Israel into the Promised Land? Fortunately, God knew Joshua was up to the task. In Joshua 1:6, the Lord commanded him: *"Be strong (confident) and of good courage, for you shall cause this people to inherit the land which I swore to their fathers to give them."* That day, Joshua had a choice. He could step out in faith and watch the Lord do the impossible through him…or he could stay in his "safety zone" and never find out. Instead of being afraid of new things, you and I ought to be excited about the new challenges and opportunities that God brings into our lives. Even when everybody else tells us it's impossible, if we will step out in faith like Joshua and follow God, He will give us the grace to go forward.

I've certainly made my share of mistakes over the years. But through all of this, I learned a valuable lesson: when we step out in obedience to God while we feel afraid, then that releases the grace (or power) of God to do what needs to be done. It is unbelievable what God can do if you'll fight your way through all the opposition that comes against you and say, "If God says I can, *I can*." It's important to remember that when the Lord calls us to do something, He also gives us the motivation and energy to press on through each challenge that comes.

Maybe you're thinking, *Yeah, I've missed a lot in my life because I was afraid to step out or fearful of what others might think.* You know what? I believe God has you reading this for a reason. You can't change the past, but you *can* begin today to follow your heart and step into the things God has for your life. Sure, there will be obstacles, and sometimes you will make mistakes. But you must be true to what God›s calling you to do if you want to be happy.

Friends, I encourage you to find and live in God's purpose for your life. Find what's going to fulfill you and all you're meant to be. Then choose to be bold enough to step out into an amazing, memorable, life-changing journey. When you step out into the unknown to do what you believe is God's will, He may not give you an exact blueprint to work with, but He *will* guide you step-by-step all along the way.

Live On Purpose

On the following pages, I want you to write the things you fear as it pertains to living on, and in, your purpose. After you write your fears, I want you to look at the objective and find the reason for your fear. Then, write down ways you can conquer your fear.

Fear: The Ultimate Purpose Blocker

Live On Purpose

Fear: The Ultimate Purpose Blocker

Chapter Five

Don't Quit

L et's face it. Sometimes things don't go as we planned, regardless of how well we plan. When this happens, we are tempted to give up and label ourselves a failure. That inner voice starts to remind you of its warning for you not to step out on faith. It brings to your remembrance how things were at least predictable when you were living your old life, before you started on this journey of living in your purpose on purpose. Yes, that inner voice gets louder and drowns out all words of encouragement and motivation to continue going.

Everyone wants to be a success. I have never met anyone who purposely set out to be a failure. Undoubtedly, this is why so much has been written on the topic "How to be a Success" and why such books are so popular. I believe it was Theodore Roosevelt who said, "The only man who never makes a mistake is the man who never does anything." The simple reality is that failure is one of those ugly truths of life—a common experience to all of us to some degree. Thus, the ability to handle failure in its various forms and degrees is a vital part of the spiritual life and another sign of maturity. A careful study of the Bible reveals that most of the great figures of Scripture experienced failure at one time or another, yet those letdowns did not keep them from effective service for God and operating in the purpose. As a partial list, this was true of Abraham, Moses, Elijah, David, and Peter. Though they failed at some point, and often in significant ways, they not only recovered from their failure, but they used it as a tool of growth—they learned from their failure, confessed it to God, and were often able to be used in even mightier ways.

The way a person meets his own failure will have a significant effect on his future. One would have been justified in concluding that Peter's failure in the judgment hall had forever slammed the door on leadership in Christ's kingdom. Instead, the depth of his repentance and the reality of his love for Christ reopened the door of opportunity to a yet wider sphere of service. "Where sin abounded, grace did much more abound."

A study of Bible characters reveals that most of those who made history were men who failed at some point, and some of them drastically, but who refused to continue lying in the dust. Their very failure and repentance secured them for a more plentiful conception of the grace of God. They learned to know Him as the God of the second chance to His children who had failed Him—and third chance, too.

The historian Froude wrote, "The worth of a man must be measured by his life, not by his failure under a singular and peculiar trial. Peter the apostle, though forewarned, thrice denied his Master on the first alarm of danger; yet that Master, who knew his nature in its strength and in its infirmity, chose him."

Understanding the amazing grace of God and His incredible forgiveness and acceptance through Christ, a mature Christian is one who has grasped the truth that his or her failure is not the end of an effective life with and for the Lord. While there may be consequences to live with (as with David) and serious issues to work through, the mature believer rests in the grace of God and uses the failure as a backdoor to success through growth and understanding.

Who will separate us from the love of Christ? Will trouble, or distress, or persecution, or famine, or nakedness, or danger, or death? As it is written, **"For your sake we encounter death all day long; we were considered as sheep to be slaughtered."** *No, in all these things we have complete victory through him who loved us. For I am convinced that neither death nor life, nor angels, nor rulers, nor things that are present, nor things to come, nor powers, nor height, nor depth, nor anything else in creation will be able to separate us from the love of God in Christ Jesus our Lord. (Romans 8:35-39)*

In view of this, we often speak of the *victorious* Christian life. But the truth is there is a lot of defeat in the Christian's life because none of us will always and perfectly appropriate the victory over sin that Christ has accomplished for us by the cross. Further, the amount of deliverance we each experience is a matter of growth; so, on the road to maturity and even after reaching a certain degree of spiritual maturity, Christians will fail—sometimes seriously so. We don't like to talk about it or admit it, but there is a lot of failure. Failure is a fact of life for Christians, but God's grace is more than adequate to overcome any situation. The mature Christian is one who has learned to apply God's grace remedy for failure.

➢ The Prevailing Attitude About Failure

Presently the bookstores are full of popular "How to Succeed Manuals" on every conceivable subject. And why is that? Too often, it is because we look at failure with eyes of scorn. We view failure as a Waterloo. We see it as the plague of plagues and as the worst thing that could happen to us. Thus, the fear of failure has many people in neutral or paralyzed or playing the game of cover up. We consciously, or subconsciously, ignore our disappointments because to admit them is to admit failure, and that's a plague worse than death. People often refuse to tackle a job or take on a responsibility for fear of failure. People believe if they fail they are no good. They think failure means you are a bad person and *you are a failure*. But, as previously mentioned, most of the great leaders in Scripture at some time in their careers experienced some sort of failure. For instance:

- When Abraham should have stayed in the land and trusted the Lord, he fled to Egypt because of the drought. And this was by no means the last of Abraham's failures.
- Moses, in trying to help his people, ran ahead of the Lord and killed the Egyptian. Later, against the command of God, he struck the rock in his anger.
- When David should have been out in the field of battle, he stayed home and committed adultery with Bathsheba and then plotted the murder of her husband.
- Peter, despite his self-confidence and his great boast, denied the Lord, as did the rest of the disciples who fled before the evening our Lord's arrest was over.

There is a fundamental principle here. Sometimes God must engineer failure in us before He can bring about success with us. Our failures are often rungs on the ladder of growth—if we will learn from our mistakes rather than grovel in the dirt. This is not to make excuses for depravity or to place a premium on mistakes or failure. This does not mean that a person must fail before they can be a success, but our failures, whether in the form of rebellion or just foolish blunders, can become tools of learning and stepping stones to success. The point is we should never allow our fear of failure to paralyze us from tackling a job or trying something that challenges our comfort zone. More importantly, we should never allow failure to persuade us to give up. Nor should we allow past failures to keep us down or keep us from recovering and moving on. This means we should never allow failure to make us think we are a failure, or that we can never change, or that we can never again walk in purpose, or that God can't do anything with us because we have failed in some way. The Bible says we are all sinners and prone to failure, but in Christ we can become overcomers.

After the horrible carnage and Confederate retreat at Gettysburg, General Robert E. Lee wrote this to Jefferson Davis, president of the Confederacy: "We must expect reverses, even defeats. They are sent to teach us wisdom and prudence, to call forth greater energies, and to prevent our falling into greater disasters."[160]

➤ Mature Attitudes About Failure and Success

(1) Mature believers understand that a Christian can become successful despite failure because of God's incredible grace and forgiveness. We may have to live with the results of some of our failures, yet God is free to continue to love us in Christ and use us for His purposes because of *grace*.

(2) The mature believer seeks to use failures as lessons for growth and change. Mature believers will act on two principles: (a) They understand that failures remind us of the weight and subsequent consequences of certain decisions. Failures remind us of what can happen; they can make us careful, but they should not be allowed to paralyze us. (b) The mature believer recognizes that our failures show us what we should and should not do; they become lessons in where we went wrong and why. You know what they say, "hindsight is 20/20." It can help us avoid the same mistake twice if we will learn from history.

Thomas Edison invented the microphone, the phonograph, the incandescent light, the storage battery, talking movies, and more than one thousand other things. It was December 1914, and he had worked for ten years on a storage battery. This had greatly strained his finances. One evening, spontaneous combustion broke out in the film room. Within minutes, all the packing compounds, celluloid for records and film, and other flammable goods were in flames. Fire companies from eight surrounding towns arrived, but the heat was so intense and the water pressure so low, that the attempt to douse the flames was unsuccessful. Everything was destroyed. Edison was sixty-seven.

With all his assets going up in smoke (although the damage exceeded two million dollars, the buildings were only insured for $238,000 because they were made of concrete and thought to be fireproof), would his spirit be broken?

The inventor's twenty-four-year-old son, Charles, searched frantically for his father. He finally found him, calmly watching the fire, his face glowing in the reflection, his white hair blowing in the wind. "My heart ached for him," said Charles. "He was 67—no longer a young man—and everything was going up in flames. When he saw me, he shouted, 'Charles, where's your mother?' When I told him I didn't know, he said, 'Find her. Bring her here. She will never see anything like this as long as she lives.'"

The next morning, Edison looked at the ruins and said, "There is great value in disaster. All our mistakes are burned up. Thank God we can start anew." Three weeks after the fire, Edison managed to deliver the first phonograph.

(3) When mature believers fail, they:

- Acknowledge their failures and refuse to hide behind any lame duck excuses.
- Confess any sin to God when sin is involved is involved in the failure.

- Study or examine what happened, so they can learn from the failure.
- Put it behind them and move ahead.

Being assured of God's forgiveness, we are to put our failures behind us, count on and rest in His assurance, and refuse to use them as an excuse for morbid introspection, pessimism, self-pity, depression, and fear of moving on.

(4) Mature believers grow through failure. They will know and act on certain truths:

- We are accepted in the Lord based on Grace, not our performance.
- We are human, and, thus, we are not now perfect nor will we ever be.
- God still has a plan for our lives. God is not through with us yet, and we need to get on with His plan.

(5) The mature believer will be one who understands there are different kinds of failure.

- **There are those who have genuinely failed per the principles of Scripture.** If we fail to know why we believe what we believe and then fail to give an adequate reason to those who ask for a reason for our hope (*1 Pet. 3:15*), then we have failed in our responsibility to witness. That can become a stepping stone to getting equipped and to becoming bold in our witness, but at that point there was failure.
- **There is a false guilt of failure because of a wrong view of success.** Many missionaries have labored faithfully in foreign countries without much success by way of converts, but that by no means indicates they are failures. A biblical

illustration is Isaiah. Right from the beginning, after seeing the Lord high and lifted up, after confessing his own sin and that of his nation, and after saying, "Here am I, send me," God sent him to preach to a people who would not listen and told him so beforehand *(Isa. 6:8-10)*. In the eyes of people, he was a failure, but not in God's eyes.

- **There is another class of failure; those who mistakenly believe they are successes!** These believers may earn an honest living and be fine supporters of the church. They unconsciously (or sometimes all too consciously) consider themselves examples for others to follow. Yet they do not realize that from God's perspective they are failures. One man put it this way: "I climbed the ladder of success only to discover that my ladder was leaning against the wrong wall!" Heaven, I believe, will be filled with surprises. Many "successful" Christians will be nobodies, and some whose lives were sprinkled with the wreckage of one failure after another will be great in the kingdom.

(6) The mature believer is one who understands the importance of choosing the right standard of measurement to determine success and failure. There are a number of common worldly beliefs about success that people apply to themselves and others, but they are all distortions of the truth. Most of these are based on some form of faulty comparison. To those who were guilty of this kind of foolishness, the apostle Paul wrote: "For we would not dare to classify or compare ourselves with some of those who recommend themselves. But when they measure themselves by themselves and compare themselves with themselves, they are **without understanding**" *(2 Cor. 10:12)*.

Fundamentally, this is the distortion of comparing ourselves with others. We are all to do our best according the abilities God has given us, and we are right in using others as models of Christ-like character. Paul told the Corinthians, "Be imitators of me as I also am of Christ" (*1 Cor. 11:1*). But this is not the same as when we compare ourselves with other people from the standpoint of their gifts, abilities, bank accounts, possessions, position, and other such standards and then attempt to determine our success or failure or that of someone else based on such comparisons. If money is a basis of judging success or failure, it is obvious that Jesus Christ was a failure. Consider this: when He had to pay taxes, He asked Peter to find a coin in a fish's mouth. Why? He didn't have a coin of His own. Christ was born under the shelter of a stable's roof. Most of us would be appalled if our children could not be born in a modern hospital. When He died, the soldiers cast lots for His garment. *That* was all He owned of this world's goods. He died naked, in the presence of gawking bystanders.

Was Christ a failure? Yes, if money is the standard by which He is judged. The foxes have holes, the birds of the air have nests, but the Son of man did not have a place He could call home. Of course, earning money (and even saving some) is both legitimate and necessary. But the amount we earn is not a barometer of God's blessing. And I might add, lots of money and things are never an evidence of success in God's eyes. Many who are wealthy are failures from God's viewpoint. The point, then, is the absence or presence of money is not in itself proof of success or failure.

The comparison game reaches out to almost every area of life. It may involve comparing friends, i.e., name-dropping to suggest that one is successful because he runs with the right people. Or it may involve believers comparing the size of their church, the size of their mission's budget, the number of books one has had published, etc. None of these things are in themselves a proof of success in God's eyes. A classic illustration is when Moses struck the rock when God had told him to only speak to the rock.

Water flowed. The people were jubilant. Was Moses a success? Yes, in the eyes of men. Not in the eyes of God. His disobedience brought water, but it also brought punishment. Results in themselves are not a proof that God is pleased. It is possible to win attendance contests and disseminate the Gospel and see results; all these activities can be done without pleasing God. Such results can be achieved by deceptive gimmicks or for purely personal satisfaction. It is not enough to do God's work and live per the purpose you were created for; it must be done in His way and for His credit.

There are many causes for failure. Some are the product of specific acts of sin, but some are not. Some are simply the product of ignorance or of circumstances beyond our control like a drop in the stock market or extreme weather conditions (drought, floods), which can cause a farmer or rancher to lose his shirt, as they say. Naturally, this kind of failure, as serious and painful as it is, is not as serious as spiritual failure like, for instance, the sin of David. While David did recover from his sin and was still used of God afterward, there were lifelong consequences in his life and in the lives of others.

Whether caused by sin or by the many things that can happen beyond our control, all failure teaches us the important truth of just how desperately we need God and His mercy and grace in our lives. Sometimes our failures are mirrors of reproof, but always they can become tools for growth and deeper levels of trust and commitment to God if we will respond to them as such rather than rebel and become hardened through the difficulty. God is adequate for all kinds of failure. Some failures may not be our fault, but they serve as reminders that we must live with eternal priorities in mind.

Regardless, God has made more than adequate provision for us in Christ and His finished work on the cross, which is the sole basis of our relationship and forgiveness with God and our means of a meaningful and productive life with Him.

In closing, I want to share with you a story I read. The story was about a man who was the sole survivor of a shipwreck who was stranded on a small desert island with only the items from his ship that had washed up on the shore with him. The man carefully constructed a small hut to store his few precious belongings and to protect himself from the weather. One day, as he was standing in the ocean fishing for his next meal, he turned back to shore to see that his hut was on fire with smoke billowing into the air. The worst was happening. "God, how could you do this to me?" he cried. He believed that all was lost. Later he heard an approaching ship in the distance. It was coming to rescue him. "How did you know I was here?" asked the man of his rescuers. "We saw your smoke signal," they replied.

"Destiny is a mysterious thing, sometimes enfolding a miracle in a leaky basket of catastrophe." – Francisco Goldman

When things in life go wrong, we often fall apart, stress out, or get depressed and sad. Yet, in that very moment, if we could step back and consider that maybe, just maybe, the hard time we are going through right now is really just leading us to the most amazing situation we could ever imagine, and what lies ahead in this new situation is going to bring us success beyond measure – if we could just trust that God truly does have a grand design for our life and that everything we are going through is meant to help us, to prepare us, to teach us, and to lead us to a situation that will create the very best outcome possible for our life – maybe then we would have the courage, strength, and fortitude to get through those tough times with a level of endurance and a hope for the future that will help us pass through those times more quickly and without so much sadness. Maybe then we could live each day feeling happy and grateful for what we are learning today and with hope for what tomorrow will bring.

***

"Your journey has molded you for the greater good. It was exactly what it needed to be. Don`t think you`ve lost time. It took each and every situation you have encountered to bring you to the now. And now is right on time." – Asha Tyson

Chapter Six

Stay Focused

The enemy's primary focus is to get you to lose your own. He will use a failure, a disappointment, or a letdown to try and convince you that you are possibly on the wrong path, and need to turn your attention elsewhere. He knows that if he can take your focus, he stands a good chance of getting you to abandon your purpose, too. As we talked about in the last chapter, a failure doesn't constitute the end. It may mean a restart. But, it certainly doesn't mean things are over.

It has proven to be very difficult to remain focused during distress or discontentment. Sometimes, no matter how hard you try, you get distracted from pursuing God's purpose for your life. Not to mention that every now and then the goals you once held near and dear seemingly slips from your grasp? You can have a purpose that begins so clear and distinct only for it to later become blurry and nondescript.

It is vital to your purpose for you to maintain your focus at all costs, and yes, even when things don't go your way.

Elijah sort of had this problem in 1 Kings 19. He had just won a great victory for God in the contest on Mt. Carmel, but instead of being hailed as a hero and welcomed by the people of Israel,

Jezebel sought to kill him. Discouraged, Elijah fled the country and seemed to have decided that he could not go on any more. This was also Jonah's problem. He did not want to preach repentance to the people of Nineveh, because he did not want those people even to have a remote chance of being spared from God's destruction. Jonah wanted God to *destroy* Ninevah. When they repented, Jonah was upset. He went out and sat himself under a vine and pouted, angry that God's way was not his way.

Also, the experience of having tried hard but not having seen very much tangible results for one's work in their purpose causes some people to lose their zeal for that work and to cut back on their work for the Lord. Maybe it has been the work of teaching, or the work of service to others, or the work of trying to encourage other Christians. If a person works long and hard and sees very little reward for their efforts, it is probably only natural to want to give up and let someone else do the frustrating work. If you have lost your zeal – however it may have happened – how do you get it back? The answer is simple: **you get it back in the very same way you got it in the first place**.

A frustrated New York attorney sits across from the "other woman," pleading for peace. He attempts to make restitution, to justify his one-night stand, to say something—anything—that will get this obsessed woman to leave him, his possessions, and his family alone. But with cool deliberation, she simply replies, "I will not be ignored." Though secular, this scene from a 1987 film contains spiritual significance. The woman, obsessed in the pursuit of someone else's husband, is completely focused on her immoral mission.

How much more focused should we be in pursuing our divine destinies? For this character, only death could stop her. What is stopping you? While this woman had a fatal attraction, many Christians today suffer from fatal distractions. Fatal distractions detour us from growing spiritually and fulfilling our purpose in life. And while it is easy to list the many external diversions that cause us to lose focus—busy schedules, difficult people, lack of money—the disturbing reality is simply this: Our most fatal distraction lives within.

It's the person you see as you brush your teeth, the one who stares at you in the mirrored glass of corporate America, and the one who goes with you to pick the kids up after school. It's even the person who accompanies you to the office, and the one who intercedes in times of intense warfare.

As the 1950s-political cartoon character Pogo stated: *"We have met the enemy, and it is us."* The apostle Paul expressed the same sentiment as he closed Romans 7, elegiac: "I love to do God's will so far as my new nature is concerned; but there is something else deep within me, in my lower nature, that is at war with my mind and wins the fight and makes me a slave to the sin that is still within me...Who will free me from my slavery to this deadly lower nature? Thank God. It has been done by Jesus Christ our Lord. He has set me free" *(vv. 22-25, The Living Bible, emphasis added).*

Often our fatal distractions are rooted in our minds. What else would explain King Saul's fatal distraction, the jealousy of his armor bearer, David? When the two returned from battling Goliath, women praised the war effort in song, saying, "Saul has slain his thousands, and David his ten thousands." *(1 Sam. 18:7, NKJV).* It was, at that moment, that Saul allowed the seed of distraction to awaken in his mind. "Then Saul was very angry, and the saying displeased him; and he said, 'They have ascribed to David ten thousands, and to me they have ascribed only thousands. Now what more can he have but the kingdom? So Saul [jealously] eyed David from that day forward" *(1 Sam. 18:8-9).*

Like so many of us, Saul's fatal distraction did not come from external forces. It wasn't the women, David, or even the lyrics of the song. Saul's jealousy was his fatal distraction, and it caused him to disqualify himself from serving as king. Saul is the only one who could have changed this negative thought process, and the same is true of us. If we do not truly believe what God has said about us, fatal distractions will come to weed out our faith.

What is distracting you from seeing yourself in the reflection and image of Christ? Is it doubt, a poor self-concept, or lack of intimacy with Christ? What do you believe about yourself? What do you believe about your potential? Beyond your scripted, religious response to friends or family, what do you truly believe about your service? As Proverbs 23:7 declares, *"For as he thinks in his heart, so is he."*

If you've been fatally distracted, there is hope. God wants you to regain your focus and pursue His original plan and purpose for your life. To do that, you must stay faithful to the things of God and obey His Word. Stay committed to the call of God on your life, be unshaken in your faith, and remain steadfast in your Christian walk.

Like the woman with the fatal attraction, like the Canaanite woman mentioned earlier, doggedly pursue your destiny. Instead of being fatally distracted, stay eternally focused on fulfilling His will.

If you tend to obsess over what is *not* working, you're not alone. We're drawn to place our attention on what isn't working in hopes to get rid of the problem. However, the more time you spend thinking about your failure or problem, the worse you'll feel about yourself and the less time you'll have to devise a solution.

When things go wrong, ask yourself the following two questions:

1. What have I learned about myself / my career / my business?
2. What can I do today to avoid the same result in the future?

The answers to these questions will help you shift to problem-solving mode. And that is precisely what I would like for you to do right now. Yes, right now. I want you to follow these steps so you can regain your focus (if you've lost it or are losing it). Maybe you are yet to encounter distractions, in which case, you can skip to the next chapter. But for those who have had issues with staying focused, the following practical tips will help you realign with the zeal you once had for living on purpose.

1. Give yourself permission to succeed.

If you haven't truly given yourself permission to enjoy success, you'll be placing roadblocks along your path to lifelong achievement. It is easy to become distracted when you haven't committed to achieving your goals with both your head and your heart.

2. Decide what is important to you.

Have you noticed that you always seem to stay focused on those things that are most meaningful to you? If you're not staying focused on the task at hand, it may be time to reprioritize what is important.

3. Write goals that motivate to you.

Do your goals motivate you? If not, it is imperative that you rethink your goals.

4. Develop a workable plan of action.

It's easy to become distracted when you don't have a well-thought-out plan of action. It is worth taking the time to write out a month-to-month plan for achieving your long-term and short-term goals. It's also worth the time to write an effective and reasonable daily to-do list – a list that will help you remain focused on going forward one bite-sized piece at a time.

5. Be accountable.

Find an accountability partner. Find someone who is willing to check in with you and support your progress. Research shows that you'll probably accomplish more if you have someone with whom you are accountable.

Your purpose is what you can't live without and what can't live without you. You have something to contribute. The little things shouldn't be allowed to get in the way of it. A vision has kept people alive through the harshest of conditions and driven others to the peak of greatness. With a clear picture of your destination, all levels of goals suddenly become more possible and within closer reach. A good vision helps you weed out the things that don't fit in the picture.

Remember that our lives are not stagnant as we are always shifting and changing. So, make it a daily practice to review, re-organize (if necessary), and you will be sure you are always moving forward decisively. Remember, your circumstances today are a direct result of your past thoughts and beliefs, which direct your actions, which creates a certain result. If you start thinking and acting in a different way today, you will create different results tomorrow.

Say these daily confessions with me:

- I WLL HAVE NO MORE DISTRACTIONS.
- I WILL NOT ALLOW DOUBT TO CREEP INTO MY SPIRIT.
- I WILL PROSPER IN MY PURPOSE.
- I WILL REMAIN FOCUSED ON MY PURPOSE AND ASSIGNMENT.
- I WILL BE THANKFUL FOR ALL THINGS—GOOD OR BAD—IT HAS ALL SERVED A PURPOSE.
- I WILL NOT GIVE UP IN THE FACE OF ADVERSITY.
- I WILL FULFILL THE PURPOSE GOD HAS FOR ME.

Stay Focused

Write your plan of action to defeat distraction.

Chapter Seven
Renewing Your Mind

Living on purpose will require you to have the right mind. You can't take an old mindset and use it in a new place. Well, you can, but you won't get very far. Some of you have already been heavily affected by negative thoughts due to life's circumstances, and my objective is to brainwash you in this chapter. Yes, I said brainwash. Many of you reading this book need to have your brains washed because you are infiltrated with all the wrong things.

In this chapter, we are going to answer the following question.

The Challenge of Renewing Your Mind

- How can a person renew their mind?
- What help can I expect from God in changing the way I think?
- What can I do to get rid of inappropriate thoughts in my mind?
- What role do your emotions have in determining what you think about?

Our struggles may not be identical, but many Christians are caught up in major battles in their mind. The promise of 2 Corinthians 5:17 (NIV) sounds great, *"Therefore, if anyone is in Christ, he is a new creation; the old has gone, the new has come."* But when reality hits the road—we fall short—especially in our thought life. The old way of thinking has not gone away. Many still struggle with temptations in their mind—bitterness, depression, fear, hopelessness, frustrations, problems, and putting it bluntly, evil thoughts—all of which hinders them in living on purpose for the purpose they were created. To be a successful Christian means to follow Jesus, to obey His teachings, to love others, to grow spiritually. But this battle still rages in the mind. God's solution to this battle is not simply to pray more. Prayer is important, but we need to do more than pray. Romans 12:2 (NIV) goes to the heart of the problem and offers God's solution, *"Do not conform any longer to the pattern of this world, but be transformed by the renewing of your mind. Then you will be able to test and approve what God's will is-his good, pleasing and perfect will."* The promise is powerful; if I renew my mind, God has some awesome benefits and rewards.

1. I will be transformed—not just cleaned up on the outside—but completely transformed on the inside, too.
2. I will know and understand God's will for my life.
3. How many times have you said, "I wish I knew what God wanted me to do in this situation." Here is the path to knowing God's will—His good, pleasing and perfect will. Renew your mind.
4. The God of peace will be with me when I renew my mind *(Phil. 4:8-9)*.

God's Part vs. Our Part

Three significant scriptures talk about renewing your mind—Romans 12:1-2, Philippians 4:8-9, and Hebrews 3:1. All three of these scriptures say *you* must renew your mind. None say, "pray that God will renew your mind." So, when you pray, "Oh God, renew my mind," you are acting much like a child that says, "Mom, do my homework for me." Most responsible parents would say, "No."

When it comes to renewing your mind, God will do His part, but not your part.

God's Part

1. "For God did not give us a spirit of timidity, but a spirit of power, of love and of self-discipline" (*2 Timothy 1:7 NIV*). Three gifts are promised by God for every true Christian: a spirit of power, a spirit of love, and a spirit of self-discipline. God extends these gifts to His children—but, are we taking them and applying them in our lives? Self-discipline in our thoughts is a critical element of renewing our minds. God has promised to help.

2. When Jesus was preparing to leave earth and return to heaven, He specifically promised that the Holy Spirit would guide us into all truth. John 16:13 (NIV) says, *"But when he, the Spirit of truth, comes, he will guide you into all truth. He will not speak on his own; he will speak only what he hears, and he will tell you what is yet to come."* Separating God's truth from the deceitful lies of Satan can be a challenge. God promises to help; He will guide you into all truth, but you must be willing to accept His help. Jesus did not say the Holy Spirit would give you all the truth. He said He would guide you into all the truth. This clearly indicates you must be seeking the truth if you want Him to guide you. It's the same as the child who says, "Mom, help me with my homework," versus "Mom, do my homework for me."

3. God promises to bring us from darkness into light. "When Jesus spoke again to the people, he said, 'I am the light of the world. Whoever follows me will never walk in darkness, but will have the light of life'" (John 8:12 NIV). Jesus brings light into the darkness in our world. God's truth is light for us. One of the most important gifts that God has given us for renewing our mind is the Bible—His written word—a wealth of truth that clearly shows His way of thinking and how He wants us to think.

King David said in Psalm 119:105 (NIV), *"Your word is a lamp to my feet and a light for my path."* God has given us an incredible tool for renewing our minds: His Written Word. Now what are we going to do with this treasure?

4. God promises to give wisdom to those who ask.

"If any of you lacks wisdom, he should ask God, who gives generously to all without finding fault, and it will be given to him" (James 1:5 NIV). He will give generously to us His wisdom! Another incredible tool for us to use!

Our Part

When it comes to renewing your mind, God has already done His part. And He will not do your part. First, you must accept responsibility for renewing your mind. After all, it is your mind. So, what does it mean to renew your mind? We need to learn to think like God thinks. We need to get rid of our sinful attitudes; our negative, critical ways of thinking; our selfish thoughts. Renewing your mind should not be confused with thoughts that come into your mind. Many times, we cannot stop certain thoughts from entering our mind. But what we do with that thought the instant we recognize that thought—that's where our response clearly shows whether we are renewing our mind. Much of what we think about is directly connected to what we are feeding into our mind. If you put pornography into your mind, that is what you will end up thinking about.

And what goes into your mind affects your whole life. God tells us in His Word, "I want you to be wise about what is good, and innocent about what is evil" (Rom. 16:19 NIV). We need to guard our mind and not fill it with junk. This includes what we watch on TV, what we read, and the music we listen to. Romans 12:2 tells us that we need to renew our minds and the benefits we will reap if we do so. But that scripture does not tell us how to renew our mind.

The Positive Approach

The first major strategy for renewing your mind is found in Philippians 4:8-9. It contains specific steps we can take to renew our mind. *"Finally, brothers, whatever is true, whatever is noble, whatever is right, whatever is pure, whatever is lovely, whatever is admirable-if anything is excellent or praiseworthy-think about such things. Whatever you have learned or received or heard from me, or seen in me-put it into practice. And the God of peace will be with you" (Phil. 4:8-9 NIV).*

You must constantly look for God's standard, not my standard. For example, the first step—think about whatever is true. I need to discover God's standard of truth, not my perception of truth. What does God say in His Word about truth? If I am going to renew my mind, I must fill my mind with His truth. I need to read the Bible daily and meditate on it. But it is not enough to have this information in my head, I must activate it. That's the conclusion Paul gives in Philippians 4:9.

A renewed mind should lead to changed behaviour. If a thought fails the test of being true, or honourable, or right, or pure, then stop going down that path in your mind. Turn your thoughts toward God and His Word. We need to put off our old way of thinking and develop a new way of thinking. *"You were taught, with regard to your former way of life, to put off your old self, which is being corrupted by its deceitful desires; to be made new in the attitude of your minds; and to put on the new self, created to be like God in true righteousness and holiness. Therefore, each of you must put off falsehood and speak truthfully to his neighbor, for we are all members of one body" (Eph. 4:22-25 NIV).*

Renewing your mind is a process, not a one-time feat. If you realize you have fallen short, don't beat yourself up; instead, focus your attention on renewing your mind right now. Get back on the right path. If you have a real struggle with one area, find scriptures that speak to that issue. Write them down, carry them with you, and read them throughout your day. The more you fill your mind with His truth, the more it will help to cleanse your mind of the inappropriate thoughts.

A key issue here is determining what do you want to think about? Learning to think like Jesus means that you must continually make decisions in your mind. Your decisions. Your mind. God won't decide for you. You must want to change the way you think. Joseph in the Old Testament was sold as a slave by his brothers. He ended up in Egypt, and eventually in prison—with no hope for the future. But God rescued him. Nowhere do you read of Joseph being bitter because of the injustice he suffered. Many years later, his brothers fear he still plans revenge for their evil actions. The response of Joseph shows a truly renewed mind in action. *"'You intended to harm me, but God intended it for good to accomplish what is now being done, the saving of many lives. So then, don't be afraid. I will provide for you and your children.' And he reassured them and spoke kindly to them" (Gen. 50:20-2 1 NIV).*

Battling Negative Thoughts

Philippians 4:8-9 provides a powerful place to start in renewing our mind to focus on the positive. But many of us face evil thoughts in our minds. They invade our mind without our permission. Perhaps you have been in church, singing songs of worship or listening to a message from the pastor, when in your mind a movie of sinful thoughts begins to play. *Where did this come from?* you wonder. Or maybe you face this battle as you try to go to sleep at night. You try to focus your mind on God's truth, but the evil movie continues to play in your mind. God offers another strategy we can use for these kinds of battles in the mind. *"We demolish arguments and every pretension that sets itself up against the knowledge of God, and we take captive every thought to make it obedient to Christ" (2 Cor. 10:5 NIV).*

God tells us to take on the mindset of a battle-seasoned soldier fighting the enemy. These evil thoughts are not conquered by ignoring them, any more than a soldier ignores his enemy. The soldier faces his enemy, and fights him. We must do the same when we face malevolent thoughts. We must use the strategies of a soldier and fight with passion. Satan is our enemy, committed to destroying us. This scripture points to the absolute need for us to know God's Word. How do we know if an argument or pretension is setting itself up against the knowledge of God? We must know God's truth before we can spot an error. How do we make this thought obedient to Christ unless we know God's truth? You must speak God's truth to the evil thoughts that come to you: "This is a temptation from Satan to get me to lie, or to lust, or whatever the thought focuses on. And here is what God says about that issue." And then, you need to remind yourself of the specific truth that relates to that evil thought. This is what Jesus did to combat with Satan in the time of temptation early in His ministry. See Matthew chapter 4. Jesus did not ignore the temptation, He faced it. And He quoted Scripture to respond to each temptation.

When negative thoughts come into your mind, don't try to run from them—attack them. Use the tools God has given you. Once you have exposed what you are battling, then begin to focus on the positive things God speaks of in Philippians 4:8. Bring God into the battle. Another strategy that can help us battle negative thoughts is to be accountable to another godly person. Give them permission to ask you how you are doing in the battles with your thoughts. You don't need to give them specific details of what you are battling, but you can give them a report on how successful you have been over the past few days. One of the Devil's most powerful tools is secrecy. If he can get you to keep all your battles secret, then he has a much easier time defeating you.

Focus on Jesus

Sometimes we are faced with difficult problems and confusion. The pain and frustration can drive us to the point of despair. The problem simply does not go away. What can we do in these situations that do not seem to have a solution? A third major strategy for renewing your mind is found in Hebrews 3:1 (NIV): *"Therefore, holy brothers, who share in the heavenly calling, fix your thoughts on Jesus, the apostle and high priest whom we confess."*

Some of the situations we face simply do not have adequate answers. In times like these, we can look to Jesus to fixate our thoughts on Him. Everything else might be messed up, but Jesus is not messed up or confused. He is seated at the right hand of the Father, making intercession for us. We must keep our thoughts securely on Him.

Thoughts vs. Actions

It is not enough to think pure thoughts. Philippians 4:9 takes it one step farther-we must put these thoughts into action. It's not enough to think kind thoughts—we must speak kind words and live out kindness in our actions. The prophet Jonah in the Old Testament illustrates the need for a renewed mind to impact one's behaviour. God told him to go to Nineveh and preach, but he ran from God. His actions reveal his need for a renewed mind. Jonah ended up inside the belly of a large fish for three days. He described the lessons learned in a beautiful prayer in Jonah chapter 2. He then obeyed God and went to Nineveh and preached to the city. A great revival broke out, and people by the thousands repented. The next actions and words of Jonah point to the deep problems he still had in his mind. He was angry that God forgave these people, so angry that he told God he wanted to die.

Our thoughts are revealed by our actions. In one sense, our actions speak louder than our thoughts. If we say we are a very generous person, what do our actions say? If our actions send the opposite message, then we may be living in denial or delusion and this clearly does not reflect God's way of thinking.

Renewing our minds is a challenge that may take a lifetime. God has provided some very special gifts to help us in this process. But the real key to remember this is my mind, and I must take full responsibility for renewing it. The blessings are incredible that God has promised; if we renew our mind, we will be transformed, we will be able to test and approve God's will in our lives, and we will experience His peace.

Do Your Feelings Control Your Thoughts?

Do you find it easy to think positive thoughts when you are feeling good and everything is going just great? But how do you respond when you feel depressed, discouraged, bored, or unhappy? Do you allow these feelings to control your thoughts? God has promised to give His children the "spirit of self-discipline." If you are going to renew your mind, self-discipline is essential. The call to Christian maturity is to discipline your thoughts and your emotions—to find the balance Jesus had in three areas of His life: His thoughts, actions, and feelings. "Right thinking" leads to "right actions," which leads to "right feelings." The priority is critical. If feelings are at the front, they will drive you wherever they feel like going. You've heard it said, "If it feels this good, it must be the right thing to do." But, my friends be mindful because your emotions will take you into all kinds of confusion.

"Right thinking" guides us in responding with "right actions." Right feelings may not come immediately, but they will come eventually. Accept the challenge that feeling good must have third place in your priorities. Right thinking is based on seeing each situation from God's point of view and then right actions.

Steps You Can Take to Renew Your Mind— Philippians 4:8-9

1. Choose one character trait per day or per week. The first one—whatever is true.

2. Remind yourself throughout the day that you want to do a personal check up on how well you are using this step to renew your mind. Ask yourself—what have I been thinking about today? Is it true? Or have I been thinking about something that is a lie? Have I been living with a fantasy in my mind? Am I worrying about what might happen? That's not the truth. Am I speculating on the motives or thoughts of another person? One way to help evaluate a thought is to ask yourself—If Jesus were in my shoes right now, what would He be thinking about this issue or person?

3. Consider the opposite of the trait. The opposite of truth is lies, fantasies, speculations. Ask yourself, "Am I thinking about something that is not true?" If so—you need to stop going down that thought path.

4. What scriptures will help me apply this trait to my way of thinking? What scriptures on truth speak to me?

5. After you have gone through all these steps, begin to apply more than one test to each thought. A young man sees an attractive young lady and thinks, "She is beautiful. I wonder what it would be like to be married to her?" His thought meets the "whatever is true"

test. But if she is already married, then this thought clearly fails the "whatever is right" test. This process of renewing the mind calls us to ever higher standards of filtering our thoughts and placing boundaries, so we do not go down the path of sin in our mind. Jesus made it clear in Matthew 5:27-28, that sin is not simply measured by our actions—we also sin when we embrace that thought and go down that path in our mind.

6. When you are evaluating your thoughts, bring God into the mental conversation. Breathe a prayer to God, ask for His wisdom. Quote scripture as a prayer of what you want God to do.

David's prayer in Psalm 51:10 (NIV) can be your prayer: *"Create in me a pure heart, O God, and renew a steadfast spirit within me."*

7. Talk with others about your challenge to renew your mind. Tell them about your victories and your challenges. The act of telling others can become a way of reinforcing these new thought patterns. It can also give you something positive to talk about. It's time to move beyond the weather and sports in our conversations. Do your feelings control your thoughts? Do you find it easy to think positive thoughts when you are feeling good and everything is going just great? But how do you respond when you feel depressed, discouraged, bored, or unhappy? Do you allow these feelings to control your thoughts?

We must allow God's Word, by the power of the Holy Spirit, to charge our spirits until our spirit is dominating our mind and flesh, or the world and the Devil will join forces and defeat us. By allowing our born-again spirits, empowered by the Word of God, to dominate our mind, we can bring it into subjection to God's Word and stand victorious when all hell is coming against us. When we are tempted to forego our purpose, then the enemy cannot toss us around with doubtful thoughts, or discouragement, and gain supremacy over us.

I can think of no better way to end this chapter than by using this passage of scripture: *"Finally, brethren, whatever things are true, whatever things are noble, whatever things are just, whatever things are pure, whatever things are lovely, whatever things are of good report, if there is any virtue and if there is anything praiseworthy meditate on these things" (Phil. 4:8).*

Chapter Eight
Living with Expectancy

Can you recall the first time you heard about Santa Claus? Do you remember the excitement you felt each Christmas season as you anticipated this oversized man with the big belly and white beard stuffing himself in your chimney to bring you toys? Most of us didn't even have a chimney attached to our house, but we bought into the myth because, in our childhood state, we were expert dreamers. We had the ability to travel to faraway places in our imagination. This was proven by our belief in childhood stories such as: *Cinderella, Beauty and the Beast, Sleeping Beauty, Jack and the Beanstalk, Snow White and the Seven Dwarfs, Pinocchio,* and the mystical *Peter Pan.* We looked forward to allowing our imagination to run wild through the forests right alongside Little Red Riding Hood, and I think we have all at some point pretended to eat some porridge in the chair next to Goldilocks. There was something so innocent and, dare I say it, magical about the innocent landscape of our minds as children.

When we got older, that mystical element of our juvenile imagination graduated to a more mature phase that we have termed daydreaming. When I was a teenager, I would sit with my friends for hours talking and daydreaming about what I was going to buy myself when I got older or how sweet life was going to be when I finally got out of my momma's house. Anybody remember doing that? If you were like me, you already knew what type of car you were going to drive, what type of house you were going to live in, what your husband's or wife's last name was going to be, all the way down to what you were going to name your kids. It was fun to sit and imagine these things because they gave us something to look forward to as we transitioned into adulthood.

But, then, we got older and something happened. Something knocked the wind from underneath our imagination and stripped away our ability to daydream. What used to be all fun and games turned into a borderline torturous experience each time we attempted to have the audacity to hope and believe.

Well, I can tell you exactly what happened.

Life happened.

Hopes fizzled into disappointments. Dreams became nightmares as one thing after another happened, and instead of taking the time to dream, you turned your focus to merely surviving. You started existing in life because that was easier than trying to live in purpose. It was less stressful to settle into monotony and mediocracy because at least there you knew what to expect. At least you could manage your organized chaos, and whatever happened from there would either be a plus or a minus—hopefully a plus.

I know what it feels like to take up residence in complacency and have absolutely no expectation of anyone or anything. With expectation comes potential heartbreak, so you spare yourself the possibility of feeling any more pain than you already have and wish for the best outcome possible. But, my friends, that is no way to live. It certainly is not how you live on purpose.

Honestly, I'm not sure most people know how to dream anymore. Many of us seem to drift along, never dreaming, never longing for something better, never fighting to achieve, and never following the power of a single purpose. I am not referring primarily to getting things – new cars, new homes, the latest Apple gadget, and the like. We have garages full of things but still lack a single, compelling purpose for living. Without that purpose, we drift along as sticks in a swollen river. Think about many of the people you know. Many are after things that do not seem to matter much. They feel that life is composed of the accumulation of gadgets and devices. But if that is all life is, then life is nothing worth contending for.

To have a purpose in life is a guiding and steadying influence. What you are up to in life is one way of describing your purpose in life. Another way is to think about what you consider most worthwhile. These are the same way of asking, "Why are you living?" "What is your purpose in life?" We simply must have some overall purpose in life. Joseph Addison said, "The grand essentials to happiness in this life are something to do, something to love, and something to hope for." Those elements give us a reason to get up in the morning and to keep pursuing our dreams even when they seem out of reach. We are made to live on purpose, and to live on purpose, you must not be void of expectation.

People with a clear-cut sense of purpose can withstand many challenges, inconveniences, and difficulties that others cannot. They do not give up. These people are like the explorer Ballard who kept going for thirteen years while pursuing his dream of discovering the Titanic. People who live on purpose are like the early travelers who risked their very lives to carve out places in the wilderness for their families.

One person's mountain is another's molehill. The same hammer that tempers steel shatters glass. The difference is in the material. Thus, it is with life. An experience that might throw one person off course is hardly even an inconvenience to another. One is drifting and gets sidetracked anywhere. The other knows where he or she is headed and lets nothing interfere for long.

To live on purpose does not mean to barrel headlong through life so intensely that you miss life while trying to live. Some of life's greatest moments come as surprises that are happy opportunities that seem to signal, "Hey, wake up. Pay attention. Be in the moment." Someone has wisely observed, "Life is not measured by the number of breaths we take but by the places and moments that take our breath away."

I read of an experiment that demonstrates the difference between existing by chance and living on purpose. Processionary caterpillars feed on pine needles. They move through the trees in a long procession, one leading, the others following, each with its eyes half-closed and his head snugly fitted against the rear brim of its predecessor. The French naturalist, Jean-Henri Fabre, after patiently experimenting with a group of these caterpillars, finally enticed them onto the rim of a flowerpot. He succeeded in getting the first one connected with the last one, thus forming a complete circle, which started moving around in procession with neither a beginning nor an end. Fabre expected that after a while they would catch on to the joke, get tired of the useless march, and start off in a new direction.

But, they didn't. Instead, the living, creeping circle kept moving around the rim of the pot. Around and around, keeping the same relentless pace for seven days and seven nights until they died of exhaustion and starvation. Food was close by, but was outside the range of the circle, so the caterpillars continued along the comfortable path.

People can be like that, mistaking activity for accomplishment and movement for direction. We can follow habit to oblivion. We can be so resistant to change that we perish. If we are going nowhere, we will get there soon. In the same manner, we get what we expect to have. And to get something you never had, you must do something you've never done or quit doing due to exhaustion or disappointment.

Expectancy is the close cousin to faith. And, you know without faith it is impossible to please God. I know you think you are playing it safe when it comes to living a life without expectation, but you are also cutting it close to displeasing God. Which would you rather do? Most have no problem expecting the unexpected in a negative sense. You have experienced those moods where everything has gone wrong that could go wrong. At these moments, you have all the faith in the world in Murphy's Law that "If anything can go wrong, it will go wrong." It is no trouble at all to believe that the next disaster that is going to happen is that the sky is going to fall or the roof is going to cave in. When it happens, you say, "I told you so. I knew it was going to happen. I knew the worst was yet to come." Looking back on those situations, you may even begin to believe that there is something prophetic about your ability to predict the unpredictable. It is easy to be "a prophet of gloom and doom." After all, we expect Satan to do the unexpected to make our lives unbearable. Too often, we don't expect God to do the unexpected and redeem us from the unbearable circumstances.

God moves based on our faith. We want God to do the unexpected, but we don't expect Him too. We know that with God all things are possible, but do we believe they are probable? Our prayers are intense, but we have little expectation. Our faith is so rooted in earthly circumstances, we are unable to look up and see the handiwork of God. When God does the unexpected, we have difficulty believing what God is doing. When God answers prayer in an unexpected way, we often struggle to identify His answer.

Every time I take a flight, I think about the force of the work behind the scenes that is taking place to bring the aircraft to its intended destination while passengers are seated comfortably in their seats. That same thing is taking place in eternity to ensure our safe arrival in heaven as we speak, only it is on a much more impressive scale. Angels are being directed; heaven and earth are being moved in unexpected ways to accomplish God's will in our lives. God and His heavenly host are working around the clock making sure that everything conforms to the purpose of His will, so that He may be glorified through His work in us.

A story is told of a small town in which there were no liquor stores. Eventually, however, a nightclub was built right on Main Street. Members of one of the churches in the area were so disturbed that they conducted several all-night prayer meetings and asked the Lord to burn down that den of iniquity. Lightning struck the tavern a short time later, and it was destroyed by fire. The owner, knowing how the church people had prayed, sued them for the damages. His attorney claimed that their prayers had caused the loss. The congregation, on the other hand, hired a lawyer and fought the charges. After much deliberation, the judge declared, "It's the opinion of this court that wherever the guilt may lie, the tavern keeper is the one who really believes in prayer while the church members do not!"

When we expect great things from God, there will always be those who think we are out of our minds. We are far from being out of our minds when we expect to experience great things as God unfolds His comprehensive plan bit by bit and piece by piece before our very eyes throughout our entire lives.

What is your expectation for the future?

Are you trusting God's plan?

I want to challenge you to see it before you see it. It's okay, go ahead and believe God for greater. Did you know God has expectations too? It's written in His Word in Jeremiah 29:11, *"'For I know the plans I have for you,' declares the Lord, 'plans to prosper you and not to harm you, plans to give you an expected end.'"*

Your Heavenly Father wants to upgrade you! So, stop sitting back and taking whatever life throws at you. Dust off your dreams. Dust off your vision. Dust off your goals. I believe that He is going to do exceeding, abundantly, above all you could ever ask or think of Him to do (Eph. 3:20). Who wouldn't want that? Yes, I know you've had some difficult hardships. I know life for you may not have been a crystal stare, but there is still hope. As sure as there is life, there is hope. Start daydreaming again. Get that childlike excitement back just as you had when you knew "Santa Claus" was coming. I know it was disappointing when you found out Santa Claus wasn't real, but I've got someone much better to recommend to you. Your Heavenly Father. He may not be sliding down chimneys, but He is seated on the right hand of the Father making intercession for you, and all you have to do is delight yourself in Him, and He will give you the desires of your heart (Ps. 37:4)!

Live On Purpose

Get reacquainted with your dreams. Write them below and allow yourself to daydream.

Living with Expectancy

CPSIA information can be obtained
at www.ICGtesting.com
Printed in the USA
FFHW012253171019
55631608-61452FF